The Sound of Your Voice

A Collection of Poetry on Ones Journey Through Grief

William Fitzgerald

DEDICATION

The definition of a ruby is a precious stone. My mother, Margaret Ruth Fitzgerald, was nicknamed Ruby and she was indeed a precious stone, my rock. It is with all my heart that I dedicate this book to her. She is behind all my inspiration. I live each day knowing I am one day closer to being with her again.

ACKNOWLEDGEMENTS

One's success is never theirs alone. From the countless times I interrupted my spouse, Andrew, to listen to my latest poem, to receiving a call from my friend Donald Watson asking me where I was in the process, I was never a lonely writer. Then there is my brother, Danny Fitzgerald, who encouraged me time and time again to not be a talker of dreams but a chaser of dreams. And finally yet importantly, are the countless family and friends that have encouraged me to write, some of which I have known my entire life, and some I have never met: my beautiful online family. Thank you.

Along the sea of your journey
The waves are not meant to take you under
Rather the waves are meant to carry you
To a life full of wonder

TABLE OF CONTENTS

A Writer's Prayer

Inspire me

Set fire in me

Let the words from your heart

Flow through mine as well

Give me the stories

You want me to tell

Help me make the world

A better place

Let my readers

Be able to trace

And find You there

Inspire me

Set Fire in Me

I will be a success

Even if my words are few

If the words that I write

Come from You

May I never neglect

The gift that I have been given

And always be proud

Of everything that I have written

Inspire me

Set fire in me

O Lord I pray

Grief

The moment your heart stopped beating

Mine should have stopped as well

To continue on without you

Was to me a living hell

All the joys of life followed you

No reason they should remain

And I became a desert

Slowly dying without the rain

The Night Wind

As I step outside

The winter wind stings my face

Like a million invisible bees

I wipe my face

From the tears I have cried

As the wind startles the trees

In the dark of the night

From inside my soul

Escapes a mournful cry

You left this world

So suddenly

I never thought goodbye

My feet are frozen

But not from the wind

That has the trees askew

My feet cannot move

Because I am lost

In a world without you

Tell Me

Tell me you are ok

That as much as you miss me

You would want to stay

Tell me it would blow my mind

The things you have discovered there

The things one day I will find

Tell me the connection is not broken

That you still see me on my journey

And have heard all the times I have spoken

Tell me my broken heart will mend

That losing you was just an illusion

And not the end

Tell me

Some Days

Some days I almost forget that you have gone

And I catch myself starting for you

Needing you to be there

Some days I try to remember the way things were

And I sit with your picture in my hand

And all I can do is stare

Some days I just glide through

Staying busy, trying not to think

When thinking is all I really do

Some days I fall victim to not caring

About anything, or anyone

Just never ceasing to miss you

The Drawer

I avoided it for days

As the strength in me failed

To open the bedside drawer

For I knew what it held

Your watch that no longer kept time,

An open pack of gum

The hairbrush with your hair

Would make my heart go numb

You would die a thousand times

In this process of my grief

And my heart would fade and drift away

Like a tree's dying leaf

Keep on Going

I will keep on going

Without counting the beats of my heart

Knowing that my days may be long

After the day that we part

I will keep on going

New surroundings to find

Knowing to ever find another

My eyes will always be blind

I will keep on going

Steadily, with no sign of being lame

Knowing I am continuing as you wanted

Still to never be the same

I will keep on going

River of Tears

So many yesterdays are gone

The years have rolled on by

I could have created a river

From the tears I have cried

Like the river runs

My tears have forged their way

Across the many rocks of time

Steadily come what may

Just as the river runs in search

For the place where it joins the sea

My tears run in search

Of my heart's final plea

I know that heaven holds you now

While I hold you in my heart

And the river is everlasting

Until we are no longer apart

Fear

It walked up on me so suddenly

I felt myself tremble

I backed away just far enough

To see what this thing resembled

Its dark presence seemed to sneer

Waiting for me to break

Closing my eyes, I steadied myself

I refuse to let it see me shake

I quickly looked within my heart

Where my weapons of war are stored

There amongst the volumes

Were the words I so adored

As I sorted through my treasure

Everyone a beautiful find

There it was written

I have given you a sound mind

As I looked back at the dark presence

It began to disappear

As I finished what I was reading

I have not given you a spirit of fear

The Last Tear

You have made your journey home

Back to the creator of your soul

Although we are brokenhearted

You have never been more whole

All the longings of your heart

Have now been satisfied

And God has wiped away

The last tear you will ever cry

Last Wish

We loved you

We believe you knew

Yet the things that brought you pain

To you they only grew

No one knows what another truly feels

The heart of one can be so deep

We think we know each other because of what we share

Yet fail because of what we keep

There are lessons that we who are left behind

Are now forced to learn

As the road we have been walking

Takes another turn

As we struggle with our goodbyes

We feel there is something we must do

So we offer our last wish

That there is peace now for you

Like Snow

Like snow falling gently

From a hidden blue sky

In my grief you appeared

Sharing tears as I cried

To my knees I was brought

No strength for me to stand

Quietly you came along

Offering me your hand

You gathered the pieces

With no words ever spoken

Like snow falling gently

On a heart that is broken

Under the Magnolia

I thought I saw you last night

When I looked out from my room

You were standing under the magnolia

By the light of the full moon

I took the stairs two by two

Racing for the door

My lover from so long ago

The one my heart adored

The night wind greeted me

As I stepped outside

It seemed to me it whispered

He is not here, he has died

The old magnolia stood alone

As clouds covered the moonlight

The wind brushed against my cheek

As I stood alone in the night

The Mountains

I went for a ride in the mountains

I wanted to talk with God for awhile

Stress began to lift away

With each passing mile

I knew that he was present

He was with me from the start

But sometimes you have to get away

To hear him speak to your heart

A world full of noise

The mountains seemed to hush

Bringing peace to my mind

That was usually in a rush

My heart heard him speak

Answers to which I had searched

The beauty of the mountains

Today became my church

Morning Dew on The Rose

People who are in our lives

For just a little while

Leave us in pain from missing them

But with more of a reason to smile

For we become more beautiful people

Because they were some one, we were blessed to know

They were like the morning dew

That has settled on the rose

When the sun shines on the morning dew

It becomes a diamond on the rose

To grace the flower with a sparkle

For a short while we sadly know

For when the morning hour is gone

And the dew has faded away

The rose seems lost without it

Yet stronger in other ways

The Dream

I was walking through a forest

Down a little dusty path

When somewhere from the distance

I heard a familiar laugh

I walked a little faster

I just had to see

Could this be possible

Could this really be

Under the umbrella of trees

The path curved to the right

But no matter how fast I walked

There was no one in sight

As the sunlight poked through the trees

Lighting the forest floor

I heard the laugh once again

I could not be more sure

I called out your name

As I started to run

The forest shadows stretched out

From the lessening sun

Finally in the distance I saw you

As you turned to me and smiled

I felt that welcoming feeling

Between a mother and her child

I ran towards you

As I started to cry

When two squirrels playing chase

Happened to go by

For just a moment

My attention had been taken

It was just then that I heard

My alarm as I awakened

Little Visitor

Who is this bird on my windowsill

Who sings her song to me?

How did she know to show up now

When my heart is just debris?

She sings her little song

With little breaks for her to preen.

I feel that she is heaven sent

My little visitor that has intervened.

Mother's Day

There is a laughter that lingers in the wind

Even after all these years

And a smile that has never faded from my sight

Even through all my tears

They say that time heals the broken heart

And maybe for some that is true

But time has only made my heart ache

For another moment more with you

It seems as only yesterday

Your beautiful smile brightened up my days

And I had a place to run

When my world became too crazed

I thank God for you mom

And even though we are apart

You will never be forgotten

You are forever in my heart

The Mourner's Comfort

I could not believe my ears

When they told me, you were gone

I could not accept the fact

That God had called you home

I cannot imagine my life

Without seeing your smile everyday

But I know where you are

You would probably say,

"Go on with your life

I am fine where I am

The Lord only called me home

So I could be with him

It was time for me to go

I never questioned why

It only hurts me now

To have to see you cry

So put on a smile

And wipe the tears away

And always remember

I will see you soon one day

The Intervention

The sun was the first to appear

Attempting to shine light into my heart

Then the birds flew in with a serenade

Determined to do their part

The soft warm breeze

Brushed gently against my cheek

The trees began to sway

As if they were to speak

The blue cloudless sky gave way

So the gentle rain could fall

Attempting to reach my heart

That I had surrounded with a wall

As night began to fall

And the sun bid its goodbye

Every color imaginable

Filled the evening sky

The sounds of the night

With the moon and the stars

Was one big lullaby

To gain entry to my heart

The wall that grief had built

Little by little began to fall

When all of God's creation

Answered to their call

Still You

The first sunrise without you

Broke my heart in two

How could another day begin

And there be no you

The first sunrise without you

My heart was so confused

The sun should be in mourning

Did it not get the news

The first sunrise without you

The birds continued to sing

Did they not understand

That death had left a sting

It took a while for me to learn

What everything else already knew

Right along beside me

There was still you

The Long Night

No matter how long the night lasts

No matter how dark the path ahead

Scribed upon our hearts

Are all the words you said

Though things may seem uncertain

At times even bleak

If we grow still and listen

We are able to hear you speak

We are not left alone as orphans

Your spirit is here to keep

And guide us through the long night

Comforting us who weep

We must always remember

The battle has already been won

The long night will soon be over

Giving way to the rising sun

Continuing On

When your gentle heart could beat no more

And this world released its hold

Your spirit climbed to heights unknown

Where only God and angels stroll

In a world that tends to dim

Your light here was amazing

You left your mark, here with us

And are now with angels praising

It seemed all the joys of life followed you

No reason they should remain

And our hearts became like the desert

Slowly dying without the rain

But the time will come when the night is over

A time when our tears will cease

For we have our own mark to leave

While you await in peace

Our Angels

It has been a while

Since we have last seen your face

Since your journey took you away

To a much better place

But your memory is always present

It is at the forefront of all we do

Everything you taught us

Is what gets us through

Mother's Day is a day

To celebrate your mother by your side

For some of us, it is extra special

For an angel now resides

For even though your duties are complete

And your race has been run

Mothers only graduate to angels

For a mother's job is never done

The Sound of Your Voice

In the beginning, it came to me

When you would call out my name

Even though in a dream

Your voice was still the same

But as the years rolled on by

And the dreams became less

The sound of your voice became difficult

For my mind to access

Then the moment came

For which I had been so afraid

When the sound of your voice

My mind would betray

In even more pieces

My heart would continue to break

Death had left me heartbroken

With a never-ending ache

But then one day as I was speaking

I could not help but to rejoice

There within my own

Was the sound of your voice

When Heaven Grew Quiet (A New Perspective)

One day up in heaven

My grandmother was sitting there

Enjoying the views around her

She did not have a care

The angels were singing

As grandmother hummed along

When suddenly heaven grew quiet

The angels had stopped their song

Surrounding my grandmother

The angels declared a surprise

When suddenly before her

Her daughter appeared before her eyes

Back here on earth

My heart broken as I cried

Everyone surrounded me

Telling me my mother had died

But I know one day down the road

As my mother is basking in heavens light

Heaven will suddenly grow quiet

As my mother and I reunite

The Clock

As the clock chimes, I watch you sleeping

Inching us closer to goodbye

As the clock ticks, I sit here helpless

All I can do is cry

Lost in memories of days gone

When you would bounce on the bed to play

Ashamed, I wonder what was ever so important

That I took for granted those days

As the clock chimes, you awake

To the long notes of noon

The time of us walking in separate directions

Is coming much too soon

I wonder if you are aware of the consequences of love

That my heart will be forced to do

I wonder if you are aware that, if I could

I would come along with you

As the clock strikes the hour

I curse it quietly under my breath

Nothing will ever stop my love for you

Not even death

Extra Miss You

Bells may be ringing

Everyone in good cheer

But for some it is the hardest

Time of the year

If it is possible to miss you

More than I already do

At Christmastime

I extra miss you

Trees may be decorated

With colors that blink

But it is the one time of the year

My heart truly sinks

If it is possible to miss you

More than I already do

At Christmastime

I extra miss you

A blue Christmas

Is putting it mild

But I must stop and remember

The birth of a child

Because of his birth

And what he came to do

It will not be forever

That I will be missing you

Angels Laughing

I can already hear the angels laughing

As you begin to joke with them

You are now in their company

And left our world so dim

You held on for so long

Suffering with a joke and a smile

You taught us to live our lives

That every second is worthwhile

While we are missing you

Our sunny sky now turned to rain

It will cheer us just a little

Knowing the angels are entertained

The Storm

The troubles in my life were minor

With little hindrance as I walked

I recalled the words you spoke to me

Every morning as we talked

You always reassured me

That you would never leave

With my troubles being minor

I had no reason to not believe

But the storm clouds gathered

As the thunder roared in the skies

The sun that set so pretty

In the morning did not rise

With no sign of ever clearing

In the water I began to wade

My doubts and fears took place

Of the mornings that I had prayed

With the water now at my knees

My heart filled with fear

It was then that I cried out

God why are you not here

As the rain started to taper

The clouds began to depart

I heard you so perfectly

As you spoke to my heart

I was right along beside you

All through the storm

But your focus that use to be on me

Had suddenly been torn

Did you notice that the storm

So quickly began to clear

The moment you focused back on me

And saw that I was near

A Pebble of Hope

Down on my knees

With a tear-stained face I pleaded

I was not looking for a miracle

A pebble of hope was all I needed

As the tears flowed

I asked God to draw near

It was then that I heard him whisper

I am already here

He said when you see the sun

Rising above the mountain slope

That should give you reason

To always have hope

When you hear the bird's song

Traveling on the morning breeze

That should give you hope

Causing your spirit to be at ease

When the moon appears

To allow the day to rest

As the stars dart the sky

All to attest

That all these things continue

To find another day to start

Because their pebble of hope

Is in each beat of your heart

Life Again

Today I felt the warmth of the sun

As it seemed so much brighter

The heaviness that I have felt

Today was a little lighter

My grief has not gone away

It appears to only sleep

For the slightest memory of you

I could easily begin to weep

But today my crying was halted

By the surprise of my own laughter

Lost in a moment of joy

I did not consider it until after

That you were there in that moment

When joy fell around me like rain

I knew that grief would not consume me

There would be life again

I Close My Eyes

I close my eyes and I can see you

You are complete in every way

The world in which I am a part

Would only continue to betray

So I do not wish you back

As much as you are missed

My tears are mixed with laughter

As now I reminisce

About all of the memories

We made throughout the years

I close my eyes and I can see you

As I smile through my tears

The River

With your soothing lullaby

Run on river run

Under the moon we slept with you

Together, woke under the sun

You taught us to run our own course

For we are only passing by

Run on river run

With your soothing lullaby

Next time we visit, you will be different

But you graciously accept the change

Run on river run

We will do the same

Now

Good morning, morning

Hello there sun

What a beautiful day

That has now begun

New possibilities

With a fresh new start

We awoke to this day

We must not leave our hearts

To live in the past

For that is all behind

Nothing life serving

There we will find

Greet the new day

And to ourselves make a vow

That we will live fully today

For we only have now

God, Dogs, And Mothers

Everyone desires to be loved

And if I had my druthers

I would want the kind of love

From God, dogs, and mothers

God's love is unmatched

A true gift from above

He said there is nothing

That could separate us from his love

Dogs were sent to earth

With love that knows no bounds

Their purpose to love their humans

A love that truly astounds

Then there are the mothers

A fierce love indeed

They would give their very lives

For their child's every need

I have learned about love

From the love of these three

Unconditional love

Is the only love for me

The Old Homeplace

The old mailbox

Had not seen mail in years

Overgrown with weeds

The driveway brought me to tears

Around the bend a little

Shrouded in trees

The old house still stood

Worn and weathered in the breeze

It looked like rubble

That should have been torn down

But inside that house

My fondest memories could be found

Memories of cold winters

My mind began to recall

Cold winds blowing

Through the non-insulated walls

The old wood stove

Could not warm it up much

But mama's cooking

Gave the warmest touch

The old house saw

Its share of tears

But there was a lot of laughter

Throughout the years

One by one

Our lives moved along

And losing mama

Was our hearts saddest song

But no matter where life takes me

On this crazy race

My heart always desires to return

To the old homeplace

One last message just for you.

Masterpiece

Mountains like giants

Oceans so deep

Sunrises and sunsets

That make our hearts leap

Clouds that hold rain

For the flowers to grow

The quiet peacefulness

Of the falling snow

Scent of honeysuckles

That makes us breathe deep

The stars and the moon

Keeping watch while we sleep

Trees that have leaves

That put on a show

The sun and the water

Making rainbows

All of these wonders

And God still knew

His greatest masterpiece

Was creating YOU

Made in the USA
Monee, IL
01 April 2024

56141699R110046